MAKE ME THE BEST

SOCCER PLAYER

BY TODD KORTEMEIER

SportsZone

An Imprint of Abdo Publishing
abdopublishing.com

abdopublishing.com

Published by Abdo Publishing, a division of ABDO, PO Box 398166, Minneapolis, Minnesota 55439. Copyright © 2017 by Abdo Consulting Group, Inc. International copyrights reserved in all countries. No part of this book may be reproduced in any form without written permission from the publisher. SportsZone™ is a trademark and logo of Abdo Publishing.

Printed in the United States of America, North Mankato, Minnesota
102016
012017

THIS BOOK CONTAINS
RECYCLED MATERIALS

Cover Photos: Shawn Pecor/Shutterstock Images, top left, middle left; Shutterstock Images, top right; Wave Break Media/Shutterstock Images, bottom left; Henri Szwarc/ Sipa USA/AP Images, bottom right
Interior Photos: Shawn Pecor/Shutterstock Images, 4 (top), 4 (middle); Wave Break Media/Shutterstock Images, 4 (bottom); Shutterstock Images, 4–5 (top); Henri Szwarc/ Sipa USA/AP Images, 4–5 (bottom); Keith Nordstrom/IOS/AP Images, 7; Elise Amendola/ AP Images, 8; Manu Fernandez/AP Images, 11; Kyodo/AP Images, 13; Victor R. Caivano/ AP Images, 14; Huw Evans/Rex Features/AP Images, 17; JMP/Rex Features/AP Images, 19; Arne Dedert/picture-alliance/dpa/AP Images, 21; Michel Spingler/AP Images, 22; Martin Rickett/PA-URN:10652951/Press Association/AP Images, 25; Charles Mitchell/ Icon Sportswire, 27; Steven Kingsman/Icon Sportswire, 28; Mo Khursheed/TFV Media/AP Images, 31, 41; Sean Brown/Cal Sport Media/AP Images, 33; BPI/Rex Features/AP Images, 35; Alberto Saiz/AP Images, 36; Kerstin Joensson/AP Images, 39; Jorge Lemus/NurPhoto/ Sipa/AP Images, 42; Ryan Remiorz/The Canadian Press/AP Images, 45

Editor: Patrick Donnelly
Series Designer: Nikki Farinella
Content Consultant: Brian Kallman, former professional soccer player and founder of Fùtebol Form & Fitness (www.futebolformandfitness.com)

Publisher's Cataloging-in-Publication Data

Names: Kortemeier, Todd, author.
Title: Make me the best soccer player / by Todd Kortemeier.
Description: Minneapolis, MN : Abdo Publishing, 2017. | Series: Make me the best athlete | Includes bibliographical references and index.
Identifiers: LCCN 2016945686 | ISBN 9781680784916 (lib. bdg.) | ISBN 9781680798197 (ebook)
Subjects: LCSH: Soccer--Juvenile literature.
Classification: DDC 796.334--dc23
LC record available at http://lccn.loc.gov/2016945686

TABLE OF

CONTENTS

INTRODUCTION

For many soccer players, love of the game starts at a young age. They carry the game with them wherever they go. They don't even need a ball. Some young players make a ball out of whatever they can find. This ball could be a plastic bag stuffed with cloth. The materials don't matter as long as there's a game. Over time players develop their touch with the ball. They learn what they can do with it and how to make great passes and slick moves.

Many of the world's greatest soccer players started out that way. They went from playgrounds and alleyways to the Fédération Internationale de Football Association (FIFA) World Cup. Their hard work and practice made them into some of the best ever to play the game.

DRIBBLE LIKE

LIONEL MESSI

Lionel Messi steals the ball from his opponent and sprints up field. He seems to move faster with the ball than without it. Two defenders try to force him to the outside. But he slips past them with a clever tap of the ball. Now it's just him and the goalkeeper. Messi usually wins that battle.

Messi was born in Argentina in 1987. The year before, Diego Maradona had led Argentina to a World Cup championship. By the time Messi was 12 years old, soccer scouts thought he might be the next Maradona. Messi moved quickly through the lower ranks of his Spanish club, FC Barcelona. At age 17, Messi played his first game with Barcelona's senior team.

Messi was named best player in the world by FIFA every year from 2009 to 2012.

Lionel Messi keeps his head up and looks for open teammates as he controls the ball.

Today he is one of the best players in the world, with more than 500 goals to his name.

Messi is a skilled all-around player. But his dribbling and control of the ball really set him apart. He can continue moving forward while still doing what he wants with the ball. Some players rely on fancy moves to fake

DRIBBLE LIKE LIONEL MESSI

- Don't just rely on your stronger foot to do all the work. Using both feet will keep your defender guessing.

- Use all surfaces of your feet. This will open the door to many more moves and help you maintain control of the ball in all directions.

- Keep your head up. You won't be able to make a pass or take a shot if you're staring at the ball.

- Master your touch. Don't put too much power behind your touches in tight spaces or you will lose the ball.

- Use your body to fake out defenders and get into open spaces on the field. Change pace and direction to get away from pressure.

Even in heavy traffic, it's hard to get Messi off the ball without fouling him.

Messi's first appearance with Argentina did not last long. He was shown a red card for elbowing an opponent in the mouth just 47 seconds after entering the game.

out defenders. Messi uses pure speed and control to get past them.

If Messi doesn't have a path to the net, he can usually find an open teammate. Defenders are drawn to Messi. That opens up space for another player to get open for a pass. Messi studies defenders and learns what might fool them. If they get too close to him, Messi can touch the ball ahead and play on. In a 2007 game, he beat six defenders on a half-field run to score one of his most famous goals.

DIEGO MARADONA

Diego Maradona had many famous goals and games in his career. He showcased his dribbling skills in the semifinals of the 1986 World Cup. Maradona got the ball at midfield. Then, barely slowing down, he dribbled past five England defenders and scored. The play has been called "The Goal of the Century." Maradona's brilliant effort helped Argentina win its second World Cup title.

DRILL DOWN!

Practicing tight turns will help you change direction quickly.

1. Set up four cones in a straight line 3 to 5 feet apart.

2. Start at one end of the line and dribble in a zigzag fashion around each cone.

3. At the end of the line use quick, small touches to help get you going the other way.

4. Players should accelerate after any change of direction.

SHOOT LIKE

CRISTIANO RONALDO

Cristiano Ronaldo stands over the ball. He sizes up the wall of players in front of him. He'll have to get the ball past them to get his free kick on goal. Then there's the goalie to worry about. But even if all of his opponents are positioned perfectly, they can't do much once Ronaldo kicks the ball. If he hits it just right, it'll find the back of the net.

The referee blows the whistle. Ronaldo runs up to the ball. He puts a spin on the ball as he kicks it. It darts up and over the wall of players. The defenders jump, but they're not tall enough to block it. The goalie rushes to punch it away, but the shot is too high for him to reach. Ronaldo placed it

In his first six years with Real Madrid, Ronaldo averaged more than one goal per game.

Cristiano Ronaldo blasts a shot for Portugal during the 2014 World Cup.

perfectly in the top corner of the net. It's another goal for one of the greatest shooters ever.

Ronaldo grew up in Santo António, a town on an island in the Atlantic Ocean hundreds of miles from the mainland of Portugal. Living in that remote location didn't limit his

SHOOT LIKE CRISTIANO RONALDO

- Take advantage of every opportunity to shoot no matter what position you play. You can't score a goal if you don't shoot.

- Keep your head down and your eyes on the ball when you kick it.

- Your plant foot should be even with the ball, a few inches to the side. Don't be too close or too far away.

- Try to make contact with the inside of your laces and the middle of the ball.

- Keep your knee and chest over the ball so that the shot stays low and on net. Keepers have more trouble reaching low shots.

- Don't stop short. Continue your kicking motion all the way through the ball and land on your shooting foot.

Ronaldo keeps his eye on the ball as he approaches a free kick.

soccer talent in any way. By the time he was 3 years old, Ronaldo was playing in his yard and in alleys. He wasn't interested in other toys. He loved his soccer ball the most. He slept with it and took it everywhere.

Maybe that familiarity with the ball helped him kick it so well. At the age of 18, he caught the attention of Manchester United. The English club is one of the best in the world. They signed Ronaldo to a five-year contract beginning in 2003. Ronaldo became one of the best players in England's Premier League. He helped United win

DAVID BECKHAM

David Beckham's bending kicks were so famous that they inspired a movie. *Bend it Like Beckham* featured young soccer players who wanted to play just like him. The English midfielder was one of the world's most popular players. His career began at Manchester United, but he also starred for Real Madrid. Beckham also captained the national team of England and scored 17 goals in his international career. He scored a goal at the 1998, 2002, and 2006 World Cups. He is the only English player to have scored in three World Cups.

Ronaldo's shooting ability has helped him become one of the greatest goal scorers of all time.

three league titles. He then went to play for Real Madrid in Spain's La Liga. He kept up his amazing goal-scoring feats there.

Ronaldo has scored more than 500 goals with his club teams and Portugal's national team combined. FIFA named him the best player in the world in 2008, 2013, and 2014. Ronaldo is a classic forward. With the ball at his feet, he is as dangerous as they come. His excellent dribbling ability helps him get free of defenders. And when he gets a chance to shoot, he does it with amazing power and accuracy.

Ronaldo doesn't want to miss a chance to shoot. If the ball is played to him, he must react quickly. He is excellent at taking a single touch on the ball before shooting. Sometimes Ronaldo wants the ball to spin so that it will fly a certain way. Other times he tries to hit it with no spin. That makes the ball dart and dive unpredictably and fool the goalie.

Ronaldo is the all-time scoring leader for Portugal.

DRILL DOWN!

This drill helps you handle a ball that's rolling.

1. Position yourself and the ball at a comfortable distance from the goal.

2. Take a touch with the inside of your left foot, then shoot with your right.

3. Repeat with the first touch using the outside of your foot, then repeat with your other foot.

4. Roll the ball forward and shoot, again alternating feet.

PLAY GOALKEEPER LIKE

MANUEL NEUER

Part of being a keeper is staying focused. You might go several minutes without getting close to the ball. Manuel Neuer uses this time to study the game. He keeps an eye on the back line of his team's defense. He notes where the opposing forwards are. If he senses danger, Neuer will run into the action, acting as another defender to clear the ball away. If Neuer isn't 100 percent focused, he could play his team into danger.

Neuer has always taken his role as his team's last man seriously. In 2013–14, Neuer played 31 games for his club team Bayern Munich and lost only two of them. Then he led Germany to the 2014 World Cup title.

Physically Neuer is everything an ideal keeper should be. His 6-foot-4-inch (193-cm) frame takes up a lot of

As goalkeeper Manuel Neuer is responsible for calling out directions to his teammates.

the net. He has good speed and ball-handling skills. Neuer believes that if needed, he could play elsewhere on the field. He sometimes plays with forwards in practice. That helps him develop his kicking and passing technique.

Neuer won the Golden Glove award for best goalkeeper at the 2014 World Cup.

PLAY GOALKEEPER LIKE MANUEL NEUER

- Focus on the game no matter where the ball is. Don't let your mind wander.

- Don't just stand on your line and wait for your opponent to shoot. Get out, cut down the angle, and make yourself bigger by spreading out your arms and legs.

- Always stay in an athletic position with your knees slightly bent. Don't get caught flat-footed or you won't be able to react.

- Communicate with your teammates. You can see the whole field, so let them know if you pick out any patterns or tendencies of your opponent.

- Come out of your box to support your team when it has the ball. Help clean up any balls played over the top of your defense.

Neuer comes out of the net and leaps high to grab the ball.

With these skills, Neuer is able to help his team's defense. He also can guide his teammates from his position at the goal. Understanding the game is key to giving his teammates instructions. But his on-field guidance doesn't mean he ignores the goal line. Neuer is a solid goalkeeper who relies on positioning to make saves. With his height and reach, he makes some amazing, diving saves. But more often, he relies on his setup to be in the right place at the right time.

Neuer won his first Champions League title with Bayern in 2013.

GIANLUIGI BUFFON

Gianluigi Buffon made his debut as Italy's keeper in 1997. He led Italy to five World Cups, winning one in 2006. He saved the championship game for Italy when he tipped a shot over the crossbar late in stoppage time. Italy then won the match in a shootout. Buffon's teammates appreciate his calm and encouraging demeanor. He takes great care to guard the goal and rarely panics.

DRILL DOWN!

This drill works on developing a keeper's instincts.

1. Stand on the goal line with your back turned to the field.

2. Have a teammate line up in front of the goal and take shots from 10 or 20 yards out.

3. Have your teammate yell just before kicking the ball.

4. When you hear the shout, turn and do your best to block the shot.

5. Adjust the drill to work on different angles or distances.

PASS LIKE

MEGAN RAPINOE

Megan Rapinoe has a lot on her mind. Her team needs a goal. She's trying to plan how to make that happen while also fending off an attacker. Rapinoe uses her ball-handling skills to shield the ball from her opponent. With her quickness, she gets free. Then she can look up and find a teammate. She sees one streaking toward the goal. Rapinoe lofts a deep, crossing ball. It lands right on the head of her teammate and ricochets into the net. Few players in the world can make a pass like that.

Rapinoe always had a playing partner growing up in California—her twin sister, Rachael. The Rapinoe twins would play one-on-one basketball or soccer for hours.

Rapinoe won a gold medal with the United States at the 2012 Olympics in London.

Megan Rapinoe thinks through her options as she brings the ball down the field.

Their mother would whistle for them when it was time to come home. Denise Rapinoe still whistles for Megan, but now it's usually because she's made another huge play for the US women's national team.

Rapinoe made her international debut in 2006. As a midfielder, she doesn't often get the chance to score. But she is very capable of doing so. She had two goals in the first game of the 2015 Women's World Cup. But her

PASS LIKE MEGAN RAPINOE

- Lead your teammate with your pass to help them get free from a defender. Or pass to their feet if nobody is covering them.

- Use the inside of your foot. The ball's flight will be more accurate if you hit it with your foot rather than your toes.

- Point your plant foot at your target. The ball tends to go where that foot is aimed.

- Follow through with your pass. If the ball doesn't reach your intended target, stay with the play and try to get it back.

Rapinoe knows that you have to control the ball before you can make a pass.

signature moment with the national team was a pass in the 2011 Women's World Cup quarterfinals.

The United States was trailing Brazil late in stoppage time. Rapinoe had the ball near midfield when she saw her teammate Abby Wambach streaking for the net. With perfect timing and placement, Rapinoe launched a long crossing pass with her left foot. The ball and Wambach reached the right post at the same time, just out of reach of

Rapinoe was featured in the video game *FIFA 16*; this edition was the first time female players were included in the game.

MIA HAMM

Mia Hamm was more than just a great soccer player. She was a huge part of increasing the game's popularity in the United States. Hamm was one of the greatest American players ever. She scored many famous goals for the national team. In 1991 she played in the first-ever Women's World Cup, which the United States won. She won another Women's World Cup in 1999 and also won two Olympic gold medals. Her dribbling and shooting abilities made her a role model for all young soccer players.

Rapinoe and her teammates celebrate their victory in the 2015 Women's World Cup final.

Brazil's keeper. Wambach headed it home, and the United States went on to win in a shootout.

Rapinoe is an important force in the middle of the field. She holds the ball there and leads the attack. Her passes are vital to setting up scoring opportunities.

Rapinoe played college soccer with her sister Rachael at the University of Portland.

Rapinoe keeps the ball away from the defense. And she has the skills necessary to fake out the other team. If she needs to, she can take on a defender herself and dribble around them. And if she gets close enough, Rapinoe has the ability to score. She doesn't need much space or time to get off a quality shot.

DRILL DOWN!

Improve the accuracy of your crossing passes with this drill:

1. With a teammate, outline two boxes about 30 yards apart on the field.

2. Stand in one while your teammate stands in the other.

3. Pass the ball to your teammate in the other box so that they can control your pass with just one touch of the ball.

4. Your teammate then passes back to you. A successful cross gets one point, as does a successful reception of the cross. Play to 10.

PLAY DEFENSE LIKE

GERARD PIQUÉ

Gerard Piqué stays glued to the man he's defending. He doesn't let his opponent out of his sight. Suddenly a perfect pass sneaks through. Piqué is chasing. Aside from the goalie, Piqué is the last line of defense. He catches up with the forward and makes a sweeping leg tackle. He wins the ball and starts the attack the other way.

Piqué grew up in Barcelona, Spain, and with the exception of a few years at Manchester United, he has spent his entire life playing for his hometown team. He worked his way up through the youth teams, showing that he could play many different positions. He has helped Barcelona to multiple league titles. And he led Spain to its first World Cup title in 2010.

Gerard Piqué, *right*, specializes in physical challenges against opposing attackers.

As a boy, Piqué was a good goal scorer. But he chose to focus on defense. At 6 feet 4 inches (193 cm), he's tall enough and has good footwork and speed. Piqué can win battles in the air or on the ground.

Piqué scored the 1,000th goal in Barcelona history in 2013.

PLAY DEFENSE LIKE GERARD PIQUÉ

- Move quickly toward the player with the ball. The faster you arrive, the less time your opponent will have to make a decision.

- Don't overcommit. Run hard at the ball, but slow down quickly by chopping your feet so the attacker won't be able to dribble past you.

- Defend both sides equally when an attacker is shielding the ball from you. Or stay on one side if you want to force the ball in the other direction.

- Off the ball, keep an athletic stance and stay with the player you're marking. Always keep yourself between that player and the goal and keep your body position open to the field.

Piqué, *right*, uses his head to battle for control of the ball.

FC Barcelona and Spain's national team are both
fast-paced, high-scoring teams. They like to use quick
passes to set up goals. Piqué starts these attacks from his
position on defense. He can quickly stop an attack and
start one the other way. He can
make long and accurate passes. But
he also has the dribbling ability to
take the ball down the field.

Piqué played every minute for Spain in the 2010 World Cup.

FRANZ BECKENBAUER

Franz Beckenbauer changed the way defense was played. When
he was growing up in 1950s Germany, defenders didn't play in the
attacking half of the field. Beckenbauer pioneered the role of an
attacking defenseman. His long attacking runs stunned opponents.
At the age of 20, Beckenbauer guided West Germany to the final
of the 1966 World Cup. He went on to win the World Cup in 1974.
He also was named best player in Europe in 1972 and 1976. Later
Beckenbauer brought his knowledge of the game to the sidelines.
Although he had no previous coaching experience, Beckenbauer
was appointed manager of West Germany's national team in 1984
and guided it to the 1990 World Cup championship.

DRILL DOWN!

Work on defensive cooperation with this exercise.

1. Start with two attackers and two defenders.

2. Attacker A passes to Attacker B. Defender C marks the player with the ball while Defender D provides cover.

3. When stopped, A passes back to B. D now pressures the ball and C provides cover.

4. Work your way down the field with the defenders trying to win possession.

TAKE A PENALTY KICK LIKE

CARLI LLOYD

A match has come down to a penalty kick shootout. Ninety minutes of regulation plus 30 minutes of extra time weren't enough. Now that the other team has missed one of its penalties, US star Carli Lloyd has a chance to win the match.

It's just Lloyd against the goalkeeper. The referee blows the whistle, meaning Lloyd can shoot when ready. She starts her run up to the ball. The goalie guesses which direction she's shooting. But Lloyd goes the other way. The ball rockets into the back of the net. It's another win for the United States.

////////// **Lloyd was named a United States team co-captain in 2015.**

Lloyd was usually the most talented player on the field when she was growing up. She became

Carli Lloyd calmly approaches a penalty kick for the US women's national team.

the leading goal scorer in Rutgers University history. She played her first game with the US Women's National Team in 2004. By 2007 Lloyd was in the starting lineup at the Women's World Cup, helping Team USA to a third-place finish. At the 2008 Olympics, she scored the game-winning goal in extra time in the gold-medal match against Brazil. She scored both US goals in a 2–1 win over Japan in the 2012 gold-medal match.

Lloyd was named FIFA Women's World Player of the Year in 2015.

TAKE A PENALTY KICK LIKE CARLI LLOYD

- Establish a routine. Set the ball on the spot yourself, set up in the same place behind the ball, take the same number of steps, and do anything else that will make you comfortable.

- Decide what your target is before you kick. Changing your mind at the last second can cause you to mess up the kick.

- Keep your eye on the ball, and watch it all the way through the kick.

- Focus on accuracy, not power.

Lloyd makes one of her six penalty kicks for Team USA in 2015.

A year earlier, the United States had finished second
to Japan at the Women's World Cup. The match went to a
penalty shootout. Lloyd missed her attempt. In 2015 Lloyd
made sure that didn't happen again.

First Lloyd converted a penalty kick to help the US
team top Germany 2–0 in the semifinals. The Americans
faced Japan in the final. Lloyd had a hat trick in the first 16
minutes of the game. The Americans went on to win 5–2
and capture the World Cup. After
her big miss against Japan in 2011,
Lloyd became the regular penalty
taker for the United States.

Lloyd converted six penalty kicks for Team USA and her professional club in 2015.

MATT LE TISSIER

Matt Le Tissier was a star for Southampton in England. He was
renowned for his dribbling skills and scoring ability. He was
especially accurate from the penalty spot. When he retired in 2002,
he had missed just one of 49 career penalty kick attempts. Le Tissier
said he didn't have any special trick to his penalties. He just picked a
corner and kicked it as hard as he could.

DRILL DOWN!

Do this drill at the end of practice when you're as tired as you might be in a game:

1. Each player on your team lines up to take a penalty kick.

2. Players take turns attempting kicks against the keeper.

3. As soon as five players in a row make one, the drill ends.

4. If even one player out of five misses, the drill continues.

5. Let players yell and make noise so it's harder for the shooter to concentrate.

GLOSSARY

CLUB

The team a player competes with outside of his or her national team.

CONTRACT

An agreement to play for a certain team.

CROSS

A type of pass that goes across the width of the field instead of toward the goal line.

EXTRA TIME

An overtime period played in case of a tie.

FORWARD

A player positioned closest to the goal ahead of most of his or her teammates.

FREE KICK

A kick taken with the ball in a stationary position while the game action is stopped.

GOAL LINE

The end line on a soccer field that runs along the front of the goal.

SEMIFINAL

The second-to-last round of play in a tournament; the winner of a semifinal game advances to the championship.

TACKLE

A physical challenge intended to take the ball away from an opposing player.

FOR MORE INFORMATION

BOOKS

Hoena, Blake. *Everything Soccer: Score Tons of Photos, Facts, and Fun!* Washington, DC: National Geographic Society, 2014.

Kortemeier, Todd. *Total Soccer.* Minneapolis, MN: Abdo Publishing, 2017.

Mills, Andrea. *The Soccer Book.* Buffalo, NY: Firefly Books, 2016.

WEBSITES

To learn more about soccer, visit **booklinks.abdopublishing.com**. These links are routinely monitored and updated to provide the most current information available.

PLACE TO VISIT

National Football Museum
Urbis Building, Cathedral Gardens
Manchester, M4 3BG, United Kingdom
+44 (0) 161 605 8200
www.nationalfootballmuseum.com
This museum brings to life the history of soccer through various collections and interactive exhibits. Open daily; admission is free.

INDEX

ABOUT THE AUTHOR

Todd Kortemeier studied journalism and English at the University of Minnesota, and he has authored dozens of books for young people, primarily on sports topics. He lives in Minneapolis, Minnesota, with his wife.